# IBN JUZAY'S SUFIC EXEGESIS

# IBN JUZAY'S SUFIC EXEGESIS

## Selections From *Kitāb al-Tashīl li-ʿUlūm al-Tanzīl*

IBN JUZAY AL-KALBĪ

ISBN 978-1-944904-05-0 (paper)
978-1-944904-06-7 (eBook)

*Published by:*
Islamosaic
islamosaic.com
publications@islamosaic.com

بسم الله الرحمن الرحيم

*All praise is to Allah alone, the Lord of the Worlds*
*And may He send His benedictions upon*
*our master Muhammad, his Kin*
*and his Companions*
*and grant them*
*peace*

# TRANSLITERATION KEY

| | | | | | |
|---|---|---|---|---|---|
| ء | ʾ[1] | ر | r[6] | ف | f |
| ا | ā, a | ز | z | ق | q[13] |
| ب | b | س | s | ك | k |
| ت | t | ش | sh | ل | l |
| ث | th[2] | ص | ṣ[7] | م | m |
| ج | j | ض | ḍ[8] | ن | n |
| ح | ḥ[3] | ط | ṭ[9] | ه | h[14] |
| خ | kh[4] | ظ | ẓ[10] | و | ū, u, w |
| د | d | ع | ʿ[11] | ي | ī, i, y |
| ذ | dh[5] | غ | gh[12] | | |

1. A distinctive glottal stop made at the bottom of the throat.
2. Pronounced like the *th* in *think*.
3. Hard *h* sound made at the Adam's apple in the middle of the throat.
4. Pronounced like *ch* in Scottish *loch*.
5. Pronounced like *th* in *this*.
6. A slightly trilled *r* made behind the upper front teeth.
7. An emphatic *s* pronounced behind the upper front teeth.
8. An emphatic *d*-like sound made by pressing the entire tongue against the upper palate.
9. An emphatic *t* sound produced behind the front teeth.
10. An emphatic *th* sound, like the *th* in *this*, made behind the front teeth.
11. A distinctive Semitic sound made in the middle of the throat and sounding to a Western ear more like a vowel than a consonant.
12. A guttural sound made at the top of the throat resembling the untrilled German and French *r*.
13. A hard *k* sound produced at the back of the palate.
14. This sound is like the English *h* but has more body. It is made at the very bottom of the throat and pronounced at the beginning, middle, and ends of words.

# CONTENTS

*This page left blank.*

# PREFACE

In the Name of Allah, Most Merciful and Compassionate

Praise to Allah, Lord and Sustainer of the worlds. May the peace and blessings of Allah be upon the Prophet Muhammad, his folk, companions, the following generation, and all who follow him until the final hour.

This piece is a translation of passages from a *tafsīr* [Quranic exegesis] authored by Imām Muhammad bin Ahmad bin Juzay al-Granati (died 1340/741), entitled *Kitāb al-tashīl fī ʿulūm al-tanzīl.*

My first exposure to this *tafsīr* was when I first arrived in Damascus and attended lessons with Sheikh Muṣṭafā al-Turkmānī. I began attending in the middle of *Surat Āli ʿImrān*, and several years later I was able to cover some of the missed material with another sheikh while studying at Qalbaqjiyyah Mosque.

Ibn Juzay began his *tafsīr* with a short introduction to the various disciplines related to explaining the Quran [*ʿulūm al-qurʾān*]. One of the topics he included is Sufism. The basic concern of Sufism is the heart: knowing its good and bad qualities, how to rid it of bad qualities, and how to instill it with the good. Ibn al-Juzay explained that Sufism is "connected to the Quran since the Quran mentions divine knowledge, struggling against the self [*nafs*], and illuminating and purifying hearts via obtaining praiseworthy character and avoiding blameworthy character." He enumerated twelve topics related to Sufism which he would explain in his *tafsīr*.

I translated Ibn Juzay's introduction to Quranic disciplines, the twelve topics related to Sufism, and his commentary for *Al-Fātiḥah* in 1999. Although I edited the introduction several times over the years, I never polished up the portions on Sufism. Seeing the state of my own heart, I decided that it was time to review the material for my own sake, and to polish it up in hopes that it might benefit others.

I ask that whoever reads it pray for everyone who is connected to this translation in any way – especially its author Ibn Juzay. May He guide us to the right direction. (Amīn.)

# INTRODUCTION

Sufism[1] is connected to the Quran since the Quran mentions divine knowledge, struggling against the self [*nafs*], and illuminating and purifying hearts via obtaining praiseworthy character and avoiding blameworthy character. The Sufis have produced explanations of the Quran. Some of them were exact and skillful, reaching nuanced meanings and guidance through the light of their insight, and halting at the intended truth. Others, however, strayed into hidden meanings, ascribing to the Quran things the Arabic language does not express.

Abū ʿAbd al-Raḥmān al-Sulamī gathered what they had said in a book he named *Al-Ḥaqāʾiq* (*The Truths*). Some of the scholars said, rather, that it is *Al-Bawāṭil* (*The Falsehoods*). When we treat it fairly, we say that it contains truths and falsehoods. We have mentioned the allusions [*ishārāt*] of the Sufis that are deemed good in a book, without those that are disputed or rejected as objectionable.

We, too, spoke of twelve stations of Sufism where they occur in the Quran. We spoke about

1. Thanks [*shukr*] at "Praise is [owed] to Allah, Lord of the worlds," [Q1:2] because of the meaning shared between thanks and praise;

2. Godfearingness [*taqwā*] at "This is the Book about which there is no doubt, a guidance for those conscious of Allah," [Q2:2];

3. Remembrance [*dhikr*] at "So remember Me; I will remember you," [Q2:152];

4. Patience [*ṣabr*] at "give good tidings to the patient," [Q2:155];

5. *Tawḥīd* at "And your god is one God," [2:163];

6. Love for Allah, at, "those who believe are stronger in love for Allah," [Q2:165];

7. Reliance upon Allah [*tawakkul*] at "when you have decided, then rely upon Allah," [3:159];

8. Vigilance [*murāqabah*], at "Indeed Allah is ever, over you, an Observer," [Q4:1];

9–10. Fear and hope [*khawf* and *rajā*] at "invoke Him in fear and aspiration," [Q7:56];

11. Repentance [*tawbah*] at "turn to Allah in repentance, all of you," [Q24:31]; and

12. Sincerity [*ikhlāṣ*] "And they were not commanded except to worship Allah, [being] sincere to Him in religion," [Q98:5].

# I

# THANKS

Allah Most High says, "Praise is [owed] to Allah, the Lord of the worlds," [Q1:2].

Praise [*ḥamd*] is more general than thanks [*shukr*], since thanks exists only as a reward for a blessing while praise is a reward like thanks and [also] an initiatory exaltation. But thanks may also be more general than praise since praise is with the tongue, whereas thanks is with the tongue, heart, and limbs.

If you understood the generality of praise, then you have learned that your saying "Praise is [owed] to Allah," entails exalting Him for all He is: His majesty, greatness, oneness, might, superiority, knowledge, capability, wisdom, and other attributes. It includes the meanings of all His ninety-nine beautiful names. And it entails thanking Him and exalting Him for every blessing He gave and mercy that He brought about to all of His creation in this life and the next.

And what words it contains, which volumes would be incapable of [recording], and the intellects of mankind fall short of counting! It should suffice you that Allah made "Praise is [owed] to Allah" the beginning of His book, and the final call for the people of Paradise.[1]

Thanking with the tongue is exalting the Bestower and talking about blessings. The Prophet ﷺ said, "Talking about blessings is thanks."[2]

Thanking with the limbs is through acts: by obeying Allah and leaving disobedience.

Thanking with the heart is knowing the numerous favors one receives, solely from Allah, and as a courtesy – not because the servant deserves it.

### *Categories of Thanks*

Know that the blessings that must be thanked are innumerable, though they are confined to three categories:

1. Worldly blessings (such as well-being and property);

2. religious blessings (such as knowledge and Godfearingness [*taqwā*]); and

3. Afterlife blessings (which is being recompensed with much reward for little work during a short life).

### *Stations of Thanks*

People are in two stations regarding thanks:

1. Those thanking the blessings that reach them specifically; and

2. those thanking Allah on behalf of all His creation for the blessings that reach them all.

### *Degrees of Thanks*

Thanks is in three levels. The level of the commoner is thanks for blessings. The level of the elite is thanks for blessings, adversities, and for all conditions. The level of the elite of the elite is to lose sight of blessings due to witnessing the Bestower.

A man said to Ibrāhīm bin Adham, "The poor are thankful when given nothing, and give preference to others when they receive."

One of the virtues of thanks is that it is an attribute of Allah and an attribute of people, since His names include the Thanker (*"Al-Shākir"*) and the Grateful (*"Al-Shakūr"*).

# 2

# GODFEARINGNESS

Allah Most High says, "*Alif lām mīm*. This is the Book about which there is no doubt, a guidance for the godfearing," [Q2:1–2].

We will speak about Godfearingness [*taqwā*][1] in three sections.

***Virtues of Godfearingness***

Fifteen virtues of Godfearingness are drawn from the Quran:

1. Guidance, due to His saying, "a guidance for those conscious of Allah [*al-muttaqīn*]," [Q2:2];

2. assistance, due to His saying, "Indeed, Allah is with those who fear Him," [Q16:128];

3. protectorship [*walāyah*], due to His saying, "Allah is the protector of the righteous [*walī al-muttaqīn*]," [Q45:19];

4. love, due to His saying, "Allah loves the righteous [*al-muttaqīn*]," [Q9:4];

5. [spiritual] knowledge, due to His saying, "if you fear Allah, He will grant you a criterion," [Q8:29];

6–7. escape from distress, and sustenance from unexpected sources, due to His saying, "And whoever fears Allah – He will make for him a way out, And will provide for him from where he does not expect," [Q65:2–3];

8. ease in concerns, due to His saying, "And whoever fears Allah – He will make for him of his matter ease" [Q65:4];

9–10. forgiveness of sins and increase in reward, due to His saying, "whoever fears Allah – He will remove for him his misdeeds and make great for him his reward," [Q65:5];

11. acceptance of deeds, due to His saying, "Indeed, Allah only accepts from the righteous [who fear Him]," [Q5:27];

12. success, due to His saying, "And fear Allah that you may succeed," [Q2:189];

13. glad tidings, due to His saying, "For them are good tidings in the worldly life and in the Hereafter," [Q10:64];

14. entering paradise, due to His saying, "Indeed, for the righteous with their Lord are the Gardens of Pleasure," [Q68:34]; and

15. salvation from the fire, due to His saying, "Then We will save those who feared Allah and leave the wrongdoers within it, on their knees," [Q19:72].

***Inducements for Godfearingness***

Ten things propel towards Godfearingness:

1. Fear of punishments in the Afterlife;
2. fear of punishments in this world;
3. hope for worldly reward;
4. hope for the Afterlife's reward;

5. fear of reckoning;

6. shyness brought about by the awareness of the gaze of Allah (the station of vigilance [*murāqabah*]),[2] due to His saying, "And ever is Allah, over all things, an Observer," [Q33:52];

7. thanks for being blessed with obeying Him;

8. knowledge, due to His saying, "Only those fear Allah, from among His servants, who have knowledge," [Q35:28];

9. glorifying the Majesty of Allah, the station of reverence;

10. true love, for the saying:

You disobey God while displaying love for Him,
this, by my life, is an unprecedented analogy.
Had your love been true you would have obeyed Him
Verily the lover is obedient to its beloved.

Allah has given the gift of eloquence to whomever said:

She said – and I had asked about the state of her lover:
by Allah describe him, removing nothing nor adding.
She said: had he expected to die from thirst
and I said "Stop approaching water," he would not approach it.

### *Degrees of Godfearingness*

The degrees of Godfearingness are five:

1. The slave fearing disbelief (the station of submission [*islām*]);

2. fearing disobedience and the unlawful (the station of repentance [*tawbah*]);

3. fearing the dubious (the station of scrupulousness [*warʿ*]);
4. fearing the merely lawful (the station of abstention [*zuhd*]);
5. fearing the presence of other than Allah in his heart (the station of spiritual vision [*mushāhadah*]).

# 3
# REMEMBRANCE

Allah Most High says, "So remember Me; I will remember you. And be grateful to Me and do not deny Me," [Q2:152].

Saʿd bin al-Masayyib said, its meaning is "mention Me with obedience, I will mention you with reward." It is also said its meaning is "mention me with supplication, saying '*subḥāna Llāh,*' and the like." The exegetes of the Quran, particularly the sufis, often explain this area with phrases having particular meanings, but there is no evidence for this exclusivity. In general, this verse is a clear proof for the nobility of remembrance. And there is the saying of the Prophet ﷺ, in what he relates from his Lord: "I am with my servant in the manner he assumes, and I am with him when he remembers Me. When he mentions Me, I remember him in Myself. And if he mentions Me in a group, I mention him in a group better than them."[1]

### *Types of remembrance*

Remembrance is of types: with the heart; with the tongue; and with the two together.

### *Superiority of remembrance over other works*

Know that in general, remembrance is the most superior of actions, even if some narrations mention the superiority of other actions (such as prayer) because of the remembrance and presence with Allah Most High that they contain.

The evidence for the superiority of remembrance is from three aspects.

The first is the texts mentioning its superiority over all other actions. The Messenger of Allah ﷺ said, "Shall I inform you of the best of your actions and the most pure with your Lord, the most raising in your ranks, and better for you than meeting your enemies and striking their necks?" They said, "Of course, O Messenger of Allah!" He said, "Remembrance of Allah."[2]

The Messenger of Allah ﷺ was asked: "What action is most superior?" He said, "Remembrance of Allah." It was asked, "Is remembrance better or fighting in the path of Allah?" And he ﷺ said, "If a warrior struck non-believers with his sword until it broke and was dripping with blood, the one [steadfast in] remembrance is his superior."[3]

The second is that whenever Allah ordered remembrance or praised those of remembrance, He stipulated that it be frequent. He said, "remember Allah with much remembrance," [Q33:41] and "and the men who remember Allah often," [Q33:35]. He did not stipulate this for any other works.

The third is that remembrance has a special form which nothing else has. It is presence in the High Gathering, and arriving at [this] nearness by that which is expressed [in] what is mentioned in the narration concerning assemblies and accompaniment [*maʿiyyah*]. Allah Most High says, "I am the companion with whom one sits for whoever mentions me,"[4] and He says, "I am as My servant expects me, and I am with him when he makes mention of Me," which is agreed upon, from the hadiths of Abū Hurayrah (may Allah be pleased with him).[5] Al-Bayhaqī's version includes: "... and I am with him whenever he mentions Me."[6]

***Stations of Dhikr***

People with respect to the goal of their remembrance are in two stations:

1. For the commoner, it is gaining rewards; and
2. for the elect, it is nearness and presence.

What a great distance there is between the two! How much there is between one who takes his reward while behind a veil, and one who draws near until he is one of the elect of the loved ones!

### *Types and Fruits of Remembrance*

Know that remembrance is of many types, including: saying *"lā ilāha illa Allāh," "subḥān Allāh," "Allāhu akbar," "al-ḥamdu li-Llāh," "lā ḥawlah wa lā quwwatah illā bi-Llāh," "ḥasbuna Llāh,"* or each of the names of Allah Most High; making supplication for the Prophet ﷺ; saying "*asataghfiru Llāh*"; and others.[7]

Each litany has its specialty and fruits.

The fruit of saying *"lā ilāha illa Allāh"* is *tawḥīd*. By this I mean the exclusive *tawḥīd* [*tawḥīd khāṣṣ*],[8] since common *tawḥīd* is obtained for every believer.

The fruit of saying "*Allāhu akbar*" is glorification and veneration for the Magnificent.

The fruit of saying "*al-ḥamdu li-Llāh*" and the names whose meaning is beneficence and mercy – including as "*Al-Raḥmān*" ("The Exceedingly Compassionate"), "*Al-Raḥīm*" ("The Exceedingly Merciful"), "*Al-Karīm*" ("The Bountiful"), "*Al-Ghaffār*" ("The Repeatedly Forgiving") – are three stations: thanks, strong hope, and love. This is because the one who is beneficent is loved without doubt.

The fruit of saying "*lā ḥawlah wa lā quwwatah illā bi-Llāh*" and saying *"subḥān Allāh"* are reliance upon Allah, resigning things to Allah, and trusting in Him.

The fruit of the names whose meanings are perusing and perceiving ("*Al-ʿAlīm*" ["The All-Knowing"], "*Al-Samīʿ*" ["The All-Hearing"], "*Al-Baṣīr*" ["The All-Seeing"], "*Al-Qarīb*" ["The Near"], and their like) is vigilance.

The fruit of supplication for the Prophet ﷺ is strong love for him and upholding his sunnah ﷺ.

The fruit of saying "*astaghfiru Llāh*" is firmly ingraining [*istiqāmah*] Godfearingness [*taqwā*], and upholding the conditions for repentance accompanied by the heart's rejection of previous sins.

The fruit of the remembrance combining [all] the names and characteristics is gathered in the Singular Litany: our saying, "*Allāh... Allāh.*" This is the furthest limit, and the final goal.

# 4
# PATIENCE

Allah Most High says, "And We will surely test you with something of fear and hunger and a loss of wealth and lives and fruits, but give good tidings to the patient," [Q2:155].

Patience [*ṣabr*] is mentioned in the Quran in more than seventy places because of the great place it has in the religion. One scholar said, "All good deeds have a reward limited from ten times its measure up to seven hundred times except patience; and there is no limiting its reward." This is because Allah Most High says, "Indeed, the patient will be given their reward without account," [Q39:10].

***Miracles and Aspects of the Patient***

Allah mentions eight types of miracles for the patient.

1. Love, when He says, "And Allah loves the steadfast," [Q3:146].

2. Victory, when He says, "Indeed, Allah is with the patient," [Q2:153].

3. Rooms in Paradise, when He says, "Those will be awarded the Chamber for what they patiently endured," [Q25:75].

4. Enormous reward, when He says, "Indeed, the patient will be given their reward without account," [Q39:10].

5–8. Four others are mentioned in [this set of] verses: good news, when He says, "...but give good tidings to the patient," [Q2:155], and also prayer, mercy and guidance: "Those are the ones upon whom are blessings from their Lord and mercy. And it is those who are the [rightly] guided," [Q2:157].

The patient are from four fronts:

1. Patience when tested, by preventing the self from anger, anxiety and apprehension;

2. patience when blessed, by tying a blessing through thanks,[1] not transgressing, and not being arrogant because of it;

3. patience during obedience, by upholding it and remaining constant with it; and

4. patience during disobedience, by restraining the tongue.

Above patience is submission [*taslīm*], which is outwardly abandoning rebellion and getting angry, and inwardly abandoning disliking it.

Above submission is accepting fate, which is the self being pleased with the actions of Allah. It comes from love [as] everything that the Beloved does is loved.

# 5
# TAWḤĪD

Allah Most High says, "And your god is one God. There is no deity [worthy of worship] except Him, the Entirely Merciful, the Especially Merciful," [Q2:163].

Know that people are in three levels regarding their *tawḥīd* of Allah Most High.

The first is the *tawḥīd* of the Muslim masses, which protects one from destruction in this world and delivers one from an eternal stay in the Fire. This *tawḥīd* is to deny [that Allah has any] associates, peers, companions, children, resemblance, or opposites.

The second level is the *tawḥīd* of the elite, which is seeing that all actions originate from Allah alone. This is perceived by way of spiritual insight and unveiling, not by way of evidence [since that is] obtained for every believer. The station of the elite's *tawḥīd* fills the heart with necessary knowledge that needs no evidence.

The fruit of this knowledge is being devoted to Allah, relying upon Him alone, and casting aside all people. One hopes for nothing other than Allah and fears no one other than Him. This is because one sees no actor save Him. And one sees that all of creation in His firm, powerful grasp, while there is no matter in their hands. So one casts aside apparent causes [*asbāb*] and renounces masters [other than Allah].

The third level is to not see anything existing save Allah alone, and to withdraw from looking to created things until it is as though they have no existence. This is what the sufis call the station of annihilation [*fanā'*], meaning ceasing to perceive the creation. And one might even cease to perceive oneself or His *tawḥīd* – meaning ceasing to perceive it due to being drowned in perceiving Allah.[1]

# 6

# LOVE OF ALLAH

Allah Most High says, "And [yet], among the people are those who take other than Allah as equals [to Him]. They love them as they [should] love Allah. But those who believe are stronger in love for Allah. And if only they who have wronged would consider [that] when they see the punishment, [they will be certain] that all power belongs to Allah and that Allah is severe in punishment," [Q2:165].

***Levels of Love for Allah***

Know that the servant's love for Allah is on two levels.

The first level is common love that no believer is devoid of and is obligatory.

The second is an exclusive love singled out for the devout scholars, the friends of Allah and the purified ones. It is the highest of stations and the end of all goals. Indeed, all stations of the righteous (like hope, reliance, and others) are built upon the self's own lot [*ḥuẓūẓ al-nafs*]. Do you not see that the one who is fearful, fears for his self; and that the one who requests, seeks a benefit for his self? This is in contrast to love, since it is for the sake of the beloved and is not for some exchange.

Know that the cause of love for Allah is knowledge of Him [*maʿrifah*]. Love is thus strengthened commensurate to the strength of that knowledge, and weakened commensurate to the weakness of that knowledge.

The requisites for love are one of two matters. When the two of them are combined in one of the individuals of Allah's creation, he will be at the extent of completeness.

The first requisite is goodness [*al-ḥusn*] and splendor [*al-jamāl*].

The second requisite is beneficence [*al-iḥṣān*] and radiance [*al-ijmāl*].

Splendor [*al-jamāl*] is naturally loved, since people necessarily love what they deem good.

Radiance [*al-ijmāl*] is like the splendor [*al-jamāl*] of Allah Most High in His extensive wisdom; unprecedented creation; and His shining, illuminating, beautiful characteristics that please the intellect and awaken hearts. And the splendor [*al-jamāl*] of Allah Most High is perceived with insight, not eyesight.

As for beneficence [*al-iḥsān*]: hearts are naturally disposed to loving whoever is righteous with them. Allah's beneficence to His servants is incessant, and His benefaction toward them is inward and manifest, "And if you should count the favor of Allah, you could not enumerate them," [Q14:34].

It suffices you that He is gracious towards the obedient and disobedient, towards believers and the non-believers. Every act of beneficence attributed to someone else is, in reality, from Him. He alone, thus, deserves affection.

Know that when love for Allah is established in the heart, its effects appear on the limbs. Its effects include earnestness in obeying Him and energy for serving Him; coveting what pleases Him; delight in His secret discourse; contentment with His decrees; yearning to meet Him; and being intimate with His remembrance. Its effects include having an aversion to all others; fleeing from people; seeking solitude through spiritual retreats; and removing this world from the heart. And its effects include affection for all who have affection for Allah; and preferring Him over all others.

Al-Harith Al-Muhasibi said, "Love is that you completely submit yourself to the Beloved; then preferring Him over your self and spirit; then agreeing with Him secretly and manifestly; and then knowing your shortcomings in your love for Him."

# 7
# RELIANCE UPON ALLAH

Allah Most High says, "And when you have decided, then rely upon Allah," [Q3:159].

Reliance [*tawakkul*] is depending upon Allah to obtain benefits or to protect them once they are obtained, and to ward off dangers or remove them after their occurrence.

This reliance is among the highest of stations from two aspects. The first is due to Him Most High saying, "Indeed, Allah loves those who rely [upon Him]," [Q3:159]. The second is due to the guarantee contained in His saying, "And whoever relies upon Allah – then He is sufficient for him," [Q65:3].

Reliance can be obligatory. Allah Most High says, "And upon Allah rely, if you should be believers," [Q5:23], thus making it a condition in belief. The apparent meaning of Him saying, "and upon Allah the believers should rely," [Q3:122], is that the order is interpreted as being obligatory.

### *Ranks of Reliance*

Know that people are in three ranks with respect to reliance upon Allah.

The first rank is the servant relying upon one's Lord just as a person relies upon his trusted agent who, without any doubt, is sincere and looks out for one's best interests.

The second rank is the servant being with his Lord just as an infant is with his mother: he knows none other than her and does not seek refuge except with her.

The third rank is the servant being with his Lord just as the deceased is with his washer, having submitted his self to him completely.

As for someone of the first rank: his lot is looking out for himself. This is in contrast to someone of the second rank whose lot comes from what is desired and chosen. And he is in contrast to one of the third rank.

These levels are built upon the *tawḥīd* of the elite [*al-tawḥīd al-khāṣṣ*] that we spoke about in His saying, "And your god is one God," [Q2:163].[1] Reliance strengthens with its strength, and weakens with its weakness.

### *Using a means and trust*

If it is asked whether abandoning apparent means [*al-asbāb*] is a condition for reliance, the answer is that means of subsistence are in three groups.

The first is a means that is known with certainty and that Allah Most High brings about. It is not permissible to abandon it, like eating to ward off hunger and clothing to ward off the cold.

The second is a means that is probable, such as trade, seeking livelihood, and the like. This does not advance its doer in reliance since reliance is an action of the heart, not an action of the body, so it is permissible to leave it for whoever is strong enough to do so.

The third is a means that is far-fetched and imagined. Its performance detracts in one's reliance.[2]

Higher than reliance is resignation [*tafwīḍ*]: complete submission to the order of Allah. The person who relies upon Allah has desires and preferences. He seeks his desires by relying upon his Lord. As for the one who resigns [his affairs to Allah], he has neither desires nor preferences: instead he attributes [his] wants and preferences to Allah Most High. It is the most complete etiquette with Allah Most High.

# 8
# VIGILANCE

Allah Most High says, "O mankind, fear your Lord, who created you from one soul and created from it its mate and dispersed from both of them many men and women. And fear Allah, through whom you ask one another, and the wombs. Indeed Allah is ever, over you, an Observer [*raqībā*]," [Q4:1].

If the servant actualizes this verse and its like, he gains the station of vigilance [*murāqabah*]. This station's foundation is a knowledge and state, from which two conditions bloom.

Its [foundational] knowledge is that the servant knows with certainty that Allah observes him, is attentive of him: He sees all his actions, hears all his utterances, and knows all his thoughts. Its state is that this knowledge be bound to the heart such that it dominates him and he is never heedless of it. Knowledge without this state is not sufficient.

When the [foundational] knowledge and state are obtained, its fruit for the "companions of the right" [*aṣḥāb al-yamīn*][1] is shyness from Allah, and it necessarily causes [*mūjib*] leaving disobedience and seriousness in obedience; and its fruit for the "ones brought near" [*muqarrabīn*] is a [spiritual] vision that causes glorifying and venerating the Venerable One.

The Messenger of Allah ﷺ alluded to these two fruits when saying, "The perfection of faith [*al-iḥsān*] is to worship Allah as though you see Him, and if you see Him not, He nevertheless sees you."[2]

The statement "To worship Allah as if you see Him," points to the second fruit: the spiritual vision requiring glorification. It is like someone who sees a glorious king and glorifies him since this is necessary.

And the statement, "And if you see Him not, He nevertheless sees you," points to the first fruit. Its meaning is that if you are not of the folk of vision which is the station of "ones brought near" [*muqarrabīn*], know that He sees you and so be among people of shyness which is the station of the "companions of the right" [*aṣḥāb al-yamīn*]. When he ﷺ initially explained perfection [*al-iḥsān*] with its highest station, he ﷺ realized that most people were incapable of attaining to it, so he lowered it [to something easier].

Know that vigilance [*murāqabah*] is not set straight unless stipulation [*mushāriṭah*] and perseverance [*murābiṭah*] proceed it, and self-examination [*muḥāsibah*] and punishment [*muʿāqibah*] follow it.

Stipulation is when the servant charges himself to adhere to obedience and to abandon disobedience. Perseverance is when the servant pledges himself to do this for his Lord.

One stipulates and pledges himself at the beginning [of a matter or period of time], and then maintains vigilance until its end. Once done, the servant examines himself concerning what he had stipulated and pledged himself to. If he finds himself to have fulfilled his pledge to Allah, he express thanks to Allah. But if he finds himself to have undone what he had stipulated and violated his pledge to persevere, he punishes himself in a manner that will deter him from repeating its like again. He then returns to the [aforementioned] stipulation, perseverance, maintaining vigilance, and testing with self-examination. It is like this until he meets Allah Most High.

# 9–10
# FEAR AND HOPE

Allah Most High says, "And cause not corruption upon the earth after its reformation. And invoke Him in fear and aspiration. Indeed, the mercy of Allah is near to the doers of good," [Q7:56].

Allah joins between fear and hope so that the servant will be fearful and hopeful. Allah Most High says, "and they hope for His mercy and fear His punishment," [Q17:57].

What causes fear is knowing the power of Allah and the fierceness of His punishment. What causes hope is knowing the mercy of Allah and the greatness of His reward. Allah Most High says, "[O Muhammad], inform My servants that it is I who am the Forgiving, the Merciful. And that it is My punishment which is the painful punishment," [Q15:49–50].

Whoever knows the favor of Allah hopes for it, and whoever knows His punishment fears it. A narration came concerning this, "If the believer's fear and hope were weighed they would be equal."[1] However, it is recommended that fear dominates the slave throughout his life, thus impelling him to perform acts of obedience and leave sins. But hope should dominate him at the coming of his death, due to him ﷺ saying, "Let no one of you die except thinking the best of Allah."[2]

### *The Levels of Fear*

Know that fear is in three levels:

1. Weak, where it is a notion in the heart of no inward or outward effect. Its existence is just like its absence.

2. Strong, where it wakes the slave from heedlessness, and propels him towards setting things straight.

3. Increasingly strong until it reaches despair and hopelessness. This is not permissible, and the best of matters is the middle.

### *The Stations of Fear*

People are in three stations concerning fear:

1. Commoners fear sins;

2. the elite fear how they will die; and

3. the elite of the elite fear prior sins, since the end is built upon it.

### *The Levels of Hope*

Hope is in three levels:

1. Hope for the mercy of Allah while using an apparent means to bring it about through obedience and abandoning disobedience. This is the hope that is praiseworthy.

2. Hope accompanied by negligence and disobedience. This is delusion.

3. Hope that increases in strength until reaching false hope. This is unlawful.

### *The Stations of Hope*

People are in three stations concerning hope:

1. Commoners hoping for the reward of Allah;

2. the elite hope for the pleasure of Allah; and
3. the elite of the elite hope to meet Allah out of love of and yearning for Him.

# 11
# REPENTANCE

Allah Most High says, "And turn to Allah in repentance, all of you, O believers, that you might succeed," [Q24:31].

Repentance [*tawbah*] is obligatory for every responsible believer. Its evidence is the Quran, the Sunnah, and the consensus of the scholars.

### *The Obligatory Acts of Repentance*

Its obligatory acts are three:

1. Regretting the sinful act out of it being disobedience to Him [the Possessor] of Majesty – not out of it being [merely] injurious to a person or property;[1]

2. desisting from the sin at the first possible moment without delay or negligence; and

3. resolving that one never repeats it. Whenever it does happen, one renews the resolution.

### *The Etiquette of Repentance*

Its etiquette are three:

1. Acknowledging the sin accompanied with broken-heartedness;

2. increasing one's humility and seeking forgiveness; and
3. increasing good deeds to wipe out prior bad deeds.

*The Ranks of Repentance*

The ranks of repentance are seven:

1. Non-believers repent from disbelief;
2. those who commit both minor and major sins repent from the major;
3. those who are upright repent from committing minor sins;
4. worshipers repent from listlessness;
5. travelers [of a path] repent from the sicknesses of the heart and ruinations;
6. the scrupulous repent from the things that are dubious; and
7. those possessing [spiritual] vision repent from heedlessness.

*The Inducements for Repentance*

The inducements for repentance are seven:

1. Fear of punishment;
2. hope for reward;
3. embarrassment of being held accountable;
4. love for the Beloved;

5. the vigilance of the Vigilant One who is near;
6. glorifying the station; and
7. thanks for numerous bounties [*al-inʿām*].

# 12
# SINCERITY

Allah Most High says, "And they were not commanded except to worship Allah, [being] sincere to Him in religion, inclining to truth, and to establish prayer and to give zakah. And that is the correct religion," [Q98:5].

Here, "sincerity" here refers to *tawḥīd,* abandoning associating partners with Allah and showing off. This is because sincerity is required in *tawḥīd* and in actions. The opposite of sincerity in *tawḥīd* is openly associating partners with Allah. The opposite of sincerity in actions is the hidden *shirk* [*al-shirk al-khafī*], which is showing off [*riyāʾ*].

The Messenger of Allah ﷺ said, "Showing off is the hidden *shirk*."[1] He ﷺ said (in what he relates from his Lord) that He Most High says, "I am the one most free of need of associates. Whoever performs an action associating in it other than Me, I leave him and his partner."[2]

### *Categories of Actions*

Actions are of three categories: commanded, forbidden, and permissible.

Sincerity in commanded actions refers to purifying the intention so that it is solely for the pleasure of Allah without being mixed with another intention. When the intention is like this, the action is sincere and accepted. But when the intention is not to please Allah (such as seeking a worldly benefit, praise, or something else), then the action is pure showing off [*riyā'*] and rejected. If the intention is mixed, then it must be closely scrutinized and considered.

As for forbidden actions: if one omits forbidden actions without any intention, he has fulfilled the covenant but there will be no reward for their omission. But if one omits them with the intention of pleasing Allah, one obtains fulfilling the covenant along with reward.

As for actions which are merely permissible (such as eating, sleeping, sex, and the like): if one performed it without intention, there is no reward for its performance. But if one performed it with the intention of pleasing Allah, then he has recompense for it. Every permissible action can become a way to draw closer [to Allah] when one's objective is to please Allah. For example, if one's goal in eating is to strengthen the body for worship, or if one's goal in sex is to avoid falling into the unlawful.

# NOTES

### *AUTHOR'S INTRODUCTION*

1. The basic concern of sufism is the heart: knowing its good and bad qualities, how to rid it of bad qualities, and how to instill it with the good.

### *1 SHUKR*

1. This is a reference to verses Q1:2, and Q10:10.
2. Al-Shihāb, *Al-Musnad* (44). The better-known phrasing is "Talking about the bounties of Allah is thanks," narrated by Aḥmed (18449).

### *2. GODFEARINGNESS*

1. Ibn Juzay explains in his lexicon at the beginning of his *tafsīr* that *taqwā* (Godfearingness) is (derived) from prevention. Its meaning is fear, and adherence to obeying Allah and leaving disobedience. He also mentions that *taqwā* leads to righteousness.
2. See page 20.

### *3. REMEMBRANCE*

1. Bukhārī (7405); Muslim (2675 #2).
2. Tirmidhī (3377).
3. Tirmidhī (3376).

4. Al-Bayhaqī, *Shuʿab al-īmān* (670).
5. The phrase "agreed upon" indicates that both al-Bukhārī and Muslim included the ḥadīth in their respective compendia of rigorously authentic hadiths, in this case: Bukhārī (7405); Muslim (2675).
6. Muslim (2675 #2, #21); al-Bayhaqī, *Shuʿab al-īmān* (546, 982).
7. The text refered to several formulas by their nickname. I have translated them into their common formula. The nicknames given in the Arabic text, and their corresponding form and meanings are as follows: *Tahlīl* is "*lā ilāha illa Allāh*" ("there is no God save Allah"). *Tasbīḥ* is "*subḥān Allāh*" ("Allah is exalted"). *Takbīr* is "*Allāhu akbar*" ("Allah is Most Great"). *Ḥamd* is "*al-ḥamdu li-Llāh*" ("Praise to Allah"). *Ḥawqalah* is "*lā ḥawlah wa lā quwwatah illā bi-Llāh*" ("There is no change nor power save through Allah"). *Ḥasbalah* is "*ḥasbuna Llāh*" ("Allah is my sufficiency"). And *istighfār* refers to seeking forgiveness, part of which includes saying "*astaghfiru Llāh*" ("I seek forgiveness from Allah").
8. See page 15.

### *4.* PATIENCE

1. This is a reference to Allah Most High saying, "...If you are grateful, I will surely increase you...," [Q17:4].

### *5.* TAWḤĪD

1. "Seeing" here is not with the eye but rather with the spirit. The state described here must not be confused with the creation being part of the Creator, uniting with the essence of the Creator, or the Creator's essence being contained within a single created being.

### *7.* RELIANCE UPON ALLAH

1. See page 15.

2. Some suggest that what is intended here are means such as magic, alchemy, and treasure hunting. (See Ibn ʿAjībah's commentary for Q3:159 in *Al-Baḥr al-madīd.*)

### *8. VIGILANCE*

1. The "companions of the right" and "ones brought near" refer to different stations in Paradise that are awarded based one a believer's belief and actions. They are referred to in Q56:27–40 and Q56:11–26 (respectively).
2. Bukhārī (50, 4777); Muslim (8, 9 #5).

### *9–10. FEAR AND HOPE*

1. Al-Bayhaqī, *Shuʿab al-īmān* (996).
2. Muslim (2877).

### *11 REPENTANCE*

1. Repentance is required for an unlawful act regardless of its consequences. This does not negate that repentance may require making amends for harming others.

### *12. SINCERITY*

1. Ḥākim (7937).
2. Muslim (2985).

# BIBLIOGRAPHY

Aḥmed bin Ḥanbal, *Al-Musnad* ("Aḥmed"). Edited by Shuʿayb al-Arnāʾūṭ, ʿĀdil Murshid, et al. Beirut: Muʾassisah al-Risālah, 2001/1421.

al-Bayhaqī, Aḥmed bin al-Ḥussein, *Shuʿab al-īmān*, e.d. ʿAbd al-ʿAlī ʿAbd al-Ḥamīd Ḥāmid. Riyadh: Maktabat al-Rushd, 2003/1423.

al-Bukhārī, Muḥammad bin Ismāʿīl Abū ʿAbd Allāh, *Al-Jāmiʿ al-ṣaḥīḥ al-mukhtaṣar min umūr rasūl iLlāh ﷺ wa sunanihi wa ayyāmihi* (*Ṣaḥīḥ al-Bukhārī*) ("Al-Bukhārī"). Edited by Muḥammad Zuhayr bin Nāsir al-Nāṣir. n.p.: Dār Tawq al-Najāh, 1422AH.

al-Ḥākim, Abū ʿAbd Allāh Muḥammad, *Al-Mustadrak ʿalāl al-Ṣaḥīḥayn* ("Al-Ḥākim"). Edited by Muṣṭafā ʿAbd al-Qādir ʿAṭā. Beirut: Dār al-Kutub al-ʿIlmiyyah, 1990/1411.

Ibn ʿAjībah, Abū al-ʿAbbās Aḥmed bin al-Mahdī, *Al-Baḥr al-madīd fī tafsīr al-Qurʾān al-majīd*. Edited by Bassām Muḥammad Bārūd. n.p., n.d.

Ibn al-Juzay, Muḥammad bin Aḥmed al-Ghranāṭī, *Kitāb al-tashīl li-ʿulūm al-tanzīl*. Edited by ʿAbd Allāh al-Khālidī. Beirut: Dār al-Arqam, n.d.

Muslim bin al-Ḥajjāj, *Al-Musnad al-ṣaḥīḥ al-mukhtaṣar bi-naql al-ʿadl ʿan al-ʿadl ilā rasūl Allah* ﷺ ("Muslim"). Edited by Muḥammad Fuʾād ʿAbd al-Bāqī. Beirut: Dār Iḥyāʾ al-Turāth, n.d.

al-Shihāb, Abū ʿAbd Allāh Muḥammad bin Salāmah, *Al-Musnad.* Edited by Ḥamdī bin ʿAbd al-Majīd al-Salafī. Beirut: Muʾassisah al-Risālah, 1986/1407.

al-Tirmidhī, Muḥammad bin ʿĪsā bin Sawrah bin Mūsā, *Al-Sunan* ("Al-Tirmidhī"). Edited by Aḥmed Muḥammad Shākir, et al, 2nd ed Cairo: Sharikah Maktabah wa Maṭbaʿah Muṣṭafā al-Bābī al-Ḥalabī, 1975/1395.

*This page left blank.*

CPSIA information can be obtained
at www.ICGtesting.com
Printed in the USA
LVHW112133310519
619780LV00001B/3/P

9 781944 904050